Top 50 MySQL Interview Questions & Answers

Knowledge Powerhouse

Copyright © 2016 Knowledge Powerhouse

All rights reserved.

No part of this book can be copied in any form. The publisher and the author have used good faith efforts to ensure that the information in this book is correct and accurate. The publisher and the author disclaim all responsibility for errors or omissions. Use of the information in this book is at your own risk.

www.KnowledgePowerhouse.com

DEDICATION

To our readers!

CONTENTS

1. How will you calculate the number of days between two dates in MySQL? **11**

2. What are the different types of Triggers in MySQL? **11**

3. What are the differences between Heap table and temporary table in MySQL? **12**

4. What is a Heap table in MySQL? **12**

5. What is the difference between BLOB and TEXT data type in MySQL? **13**

6. What will happen when AUTO_INVREMENT on an INTEGER column reaches MAX_VALUE in MySQL? **14**

7. What are the advantages of MySQL as compared with Oracle DB? **14**

8. What are the disadvantages of MySQL? **15**

9. What is the difference between CHAR and VARCHAR datatype in MySQL? **16**

10. What is the use of 'i_am_a_dummy flag' in MySQL? **16**

11. How can we get current date and time in MySQL? **17**

12. What is the difference between timestamp in Unix and MySQL? **18**

13. How will you limit a MySQL query to display only top 10 rows? **18**

14. What is automatic initialization and updating for TIMESTAMP in a MySQL table? **19**

15. How can we get the list of all the indexes on a table? **20**

16. What is SAVEPOINT in MySQL? **20**

17. 17. What is the difference between ROLLBACK TO SAVEPOINT and RELEASE SAVEPOINT? **20**

18. How will you search for a String in MySQL column? **21**

19. How can we find the version of the MySQL server and the name of the current database by SELECT query? **21**

20. What is the use of IFNULL() operator in MySQL? **22**

21. How will you check if a table exists in MySQL? **22**

22. How will you see the structure of a table in MySQL? **23**

23. What are the objects that can be created by CREATE statement in MySQL? **23**

24. 24. How will you see the current user logged into MySQL connection? **24**

25. How can you copy the structure of a table into another table without copying the data? **24**

26. What is the difference between Batch and Interactive modes of MySQL? 24

27. How can we get a random number between 1 and 100 in MySQL? 25

28. What is the difference between Primary key and Candidate key? 26

29. What is a Federated table in MySQL? 26

30. How will you get the comma separated values for a column in a MySQL Group query? 27

31. How can we get the results from a table in a random order in MySQL? 27

32. How can we prevent duplicate records in a MySQL table? 28

33. How will you eliminate duplicate values from a query result in MySQL? 28

34. How will you get the size of data in a MySQL table? 29

35. What is the option in Amazon Web Services for MySQL? 29

36. How can we manage multiple MySQL servers? 30

37. How will you migrate your SQL Server database to MySQL? 30

38. What is the difference between MySQL and Oracle? 30

39. What is the order of privileges in MySQL? 31

40. Is it ok to mention a table name in lower case while creation and in uppercase while retrieving data from MySQL DB? 32

41. Why this query does not work in MySQL? 32

42. What is mysqldump? 33

43. What is the limitation of mysqldump? 33

44. Can we run Javascript or Python code in MySQL? 33

45. What are user-defined variables in MySQL? 34

46. How will you optimize a SELECT query in MySQL? 34

47. What are the different optimization techniques in MySQL? 35

48. How can we optimize INSERT query in MySQL? 36

49. How will you make MySQL system secure against attackers? 37

50. How can you protect your MySQL server against Denial of Service attacks? 38

ACKNOWLEDGMENTS

We thank our readers who constantly send feedback and reviews to motivate us in creating these useful books with the latest information!

INTRODUCTION

This book contains basic to expert level MySQL interview questions that an interviewer asks. Each question is accompanied with an answer so that you can prepare for job interview in short time.

We have compiled this list after attending dozens of technical interviews in top-notch companies like- Google, Facebook, Netflix, Amazon etc.

Often, these questions and concepts are used in our daily programming work. But these are most helpful when an Interviewer is trying to test your deep knowledge of MySQL.

The difficulty rating on these Questions varies from a Fresher level software programmer to a Senior software programmer.

Once you go through them in the first pass, mark the questions that you could not answer by yourself. Then, in second pass go through only the difficult questions.

After going through this book 2-3 times, you will be well prepared to face a technical interview on MySQL for an experienced programmer.

MySQL Interview Questions

1. How will you calculate the number of days between two dates in MySQL?

We can use DATEDIFF function for this purpose.

The query to get the number of days between two dates in MySQL is as follows:

SELECT DATEDIFF('2016-12-31', '2015-01-01');

2. What are the different types of Triggers in MySQL?

MySQL supports six types of triggers. These are as follows:

I. **Before Insert**: This trigger runs before inserting a new row in a table.
II. **After Insert**: This trigger runs after inserting a new row in a table.
III. **Before Update**: This trigger runs before

updating an existing row in a table.

IV. **After Update**: This trigger runs after updating an existing row in a table.

V. **Before Delete**: This trigger runs before deleting an existing row in a table.

VI. **After Delete**: This trigger runs after deleting an existing row in a table.

3. What are the differences between Heap table and temporary table in MySQL?

I. **Duration**: Heap tables are stored in memory. Therefore a Heap table remains in existence even if the session is disconnected. When we restart Database, Heap tables get cleaned up.

II. Temporary tables are valid only during a session. Once the session is disconnected, temporary table is cleaned up.

III. **Privilege**: We need special privilege to create a Temporary table. Heap tables are just another form of storage in MySQL.

IV. **Sharing**: Temporary tables are not shared between clients. Each connection will have a unique temporary table. But Heap tables can be shared between clients.

4. What is a Heap table in

MySQL?

In MySQL there are tables that are present in memory. These are called Heap tables. During table creation we specify TYPE as HEAP for HEAP tables.

Heap tables provide very fast access to data.

We can not store BLOB or TEXT datatype in a HEAP table. These tables also do not support AUTO_INCREMENT.

Once we restart the Database, data in HEAP tables is lost.

5. What is the difference between BLOB and TEXT data type in MySQL?

BLOB is a Binary large Object. We can store a large amount of binary data in a BLOB data type column. TEXT is non-binary, character based string data type. We can store text data in TEXT column. We have to define a character set with a TEXT column. TEXT can be easily converted into plain text.

BLOB has four types: TINYBLOB, BLOB, MEDIUMBLOB and LONGBLOB. Where as, TEXT has its own four types: TINYTEXT, TEXT, MEDIUMTEXT, LONGTEXT.

6. What will happen when AUTO_INVREMENT on an INTEGER column reaches MAX_VALUE in MySQL?

Once a column reaches the MAX_VALUE, the AUTO_INCREMENT stops working. It gives following error in log:

ERROR: 1467 (HY000): Failed to read auto-increment value from storage engine

7. What are the advantages of MySQL as compared with Oracle DB?

Some of the main advantages of MySQL over Oracle DB are as follows:

I. **Cost**: MySQL is an Open Source and free RDBMS software. Oracle is usually a paid option for RDBMS.

II. **Space**: MySQL uses around 1 MB to run whereas Oracle may need as high as 128

MB to run the database server.

III. **Flexibility**: MySQL can be used to run a small website as well as very large scale systems. Oracle is generally used in medium to large scale systems.

IV. **Management**: In MySQL, database administration is much easier due to self-management features like- automatic space expansion, auto-restart and dynamic configuration changes. In Oracle dedicated DBA has to work on managing the Database.

V. **Portable**: MySQL is easily portable to different hardware and operating system. Migrating Oracle from one platform to another is a tougher task.

8. What are the disadvantages of MySQL?

Some of the main disadvantages of MySQL are as follows:
Dependent on Additional S/W: MySQL has less number of features in standard out-of-box version. So we have to add additional software to get more features. It gets difficult to find, decide and use the additional software with MySQL.
SQL Compliance: MySQL is not full SQL compliant. Due to this developers find it difficult to cope with the syntax of SQL in MySQL.
Transaction handling: Some users complain that

DB transactions are not handled properly in MySQL.

9. What is the difference between CHAR and VARCHAR datatype in MySQL?

Some of the main differences between CHAR and VARCHAR datatypes in MySQL are as follows:

I. **Size**: In a CHAR type column, length is fixed. In a VARCHAR type column length can vary.

II. **Storage**: There are different mechanisms to store and retrieve CHAR and VARCHAR data types in MySQL.

III. **Maximum Size**: A CHAR data type can hold maximum 255 characters. A VARCHAR datatype can store up to 4000 characters.

IV. **Speed**: CHAR datatype is 50% faster than VARCHAR datatype in MySQL.

V. **Memory Allocation**: A CHAR datatype column uses static memory allocation. Since the length of data stored in a VARCHAR can vary, this datatype uses dynamic memory allocation.

10. What is the use of

'i_am_a_dummy flag' in MySQL?

In MySQL, there is falg "ia_am_a_dummy" that can be used to save beginner developers from erroneous query like 'DELETE FROM table_name'. If we run this query it will delete all the data from table names table_name.

With 'i_am_a_dummy flag', MySQL will not permit running such a query. It will prompt user to create a query with WHERE clause so that only specific data is deleted.

We can achieve similar functionality with 'safe_updates' option in MySQL.

This flag also works on UPDATE statement to restrict updates on a table without WHERE clause.

11. How can we get current date and time in MySQL?

We can use following query in MySQL to get the current date:

SELECT CURRENT_DATE();

We can use following query in MySQL to get the current time as well as date:

```
SELECT NOW();
```

12. What is the difference between timestamp in Unix and MySQL?

In Unix as well as in MySQL, timestamp is stored as a 32-bit integer.

A timestamp is the number of seconds from the Unix Epoch on January 1st, 1970 at UTC.

In MySQL we can represent the timestamp in a readable format.

Timestamp format in MySQL is YYYY-MM-DD HH:MM:SS

13. How will you limit a MySQL query to display only top 10 rows?

We can use LIMIT clause in MySQL to limit a query to a range of rows.

Following query will give top 10 rows from the table with table_name:

SELECT * FROM <table_name> LIMIT 0,10;

Following query will give 6 rows starting from the 4th row in table with table_name:

SELECT * FROM <table_name> LIMIT 3,6;

14. What is automatic initialization and updating for TIMESTAMP in a MySQL table?

In MySQL, there is a TIMESTAMP datatype that provides features like automatic initialization and updating to current time and date.

If a column is auto-initialized, then it will be set to current timestamp on inserting a new row with no value for the column.

If a column is auto-updated, then its value will be updated to current timestamp when the value of any other column in the same row is updated.

We can mark a column as DEFAULT to prevent this auto-initialize and auto-update behavior.

15. How can we get the list of all

the indexes on a table?

We can use following command to get the list of all the indexes on a table in MySQL:

SHOW INDEX FROM table_name;

At maximum we can use 16 columns in a multi-column index of table.

16. What is SAVEPOINT in MySQL?

SAVEPOINT is a statement in SQL. We can use SAVEPOINT <savepoint_name> statement to create a point of time in a Database transaction with a name. Later we can use this savepoint to rollback the transaction upto that point of time.

17. 17. What is the difference between ROLLBACK TO SAVEPOINT and RELEASE SAVEPOINT?

We use ROLLBACK TO SAVEPOINT statement to undo the effect of a transaction upto the SAVEPOINT mentioned in ROLLBACK statement.

RELEASE SAVEPOINT is simply used to delete the SAVEPOINT with a name from a transaction. There is commit or rollback for SAVEPOINT in RELEASE statement.

In both the cases we should have first created a SAVEPOINT. Else we will get the error while doing ROLLBACK or RELEASE of a SAVEPOINT.

18. How will you search for a String in MySQL column?

We can use REGEXP operator to search for a String in MySQL column. It is regular expression search on columns with text type value.

We can define different types of regular expressions and search them in a text with the REGEXP expression that can match our crietria.

19. How can we find the version of the MySQL server and the name of the current database by SELECT query?

We can use built in functions VERSION() and DATABASE() in MySQL to get the version of

MySQL server and the name of database in MySQL.

Query is as follows:

SELECT VERSION(), DATABASE();

20. What is the use of IFNULL() operator in MySQL?

We use IFNULL operator in MySQL to get a non-null value for a column with null value.

IFNULL(expr1, expr2)
If expr1 is not null then expr1 is returned. If expr1 is null then expr2 is returned.

Eg. SELECT name, IFNULL(id,'Unknown') AS 'id' FROM user;

If id is not null then id is returned. If id is null then Unknown is returned.

21. How will you check if a table exists in MySQL?

We can use CHECK TABLE query to see the existence of a table in MySQL.

Query is as follows:

CHECK TABLE <table_name>;

22. How will you see the structure of a table in MySQL?

We can use DESC query to see the structure of a table in MySQL. It will return the name of columns and their datatype in a table.

Query is as follows:

DESC <table_name>;

23. What are the objects that can be created by CREATE statement in MySQL?

We can create following objects by CREATE statement in MySQL:

DATABASE
USER
TABLE
INDEX
VIEW
TRIGGER
EVENT
FUNCTION
PROCEDURE

24. 24. How will you see the current user logged into MySQL connection?

We can use USER() command to get the user logged into MySQL connection.

Command is as follows:

SELECT USER();

25. How can you copy the structure of a table into another table without copying the data?

It is a trick question. But it has practical use in day to day work.

Query for this is as follows:
CREATE TABLE table_name AS SELECT * FROM USER WHERE 1 > 2;

In this example condition in WHERE clause will be always false. Due to this no data is retrieved by SELECT query.

26. What is the difference between Batch and Interactive modes of MySQL?

In Interactive mode, we use command line interface and enter queries one by one. MySQL will execute the query and return the result in command line interface.

In Batch mode of MySQL we can write all the queries in a SQL file. Then we can run this SQL file from MySQL command line or from Scheduler Job. MySQL will execute all the queries and return the result.

27. How can we get a random number between 1 and 100 in MySQL?

In MySQL we have a RAND() function that returns a random number between 0 and 1.

SELECT RAND();

If we want to get a random number between 1 and 100, we can use following query:

SELECT RAND() * 100;

28. What is the difference between

Primary key and Candidate key?

We use Primary key to uniquely identify a row in a table. There is only one Primary key in a table.

There can be other keys in a table that uniquely identify a row. But they all may not be labelled as a Primary key.

All the keys that are candidate for a primary key are called Candidate key.

29. What is a Federated table in MySQL?

A Federated table in MySQL is same as any other table. The only difference is that a Federated table points to a table in another MySQl Database instance. The other MySQL database instance may live on a different host as well.

Federated table is similar to DB Link in Oracle database.

30. How will you get the comma separated values for a column in a MySQL Group query?

MySQL provides a function GROUP_CONCAT() that returns the concatenated non-null values for a group in GROUP BY query.

Eg. If there is a Employee table with Dept column. We can run a GROUP BY query on Dept column and get the list employees name in a comma-separated format.

SELECT DEPT, GROUP_CONCAT(EMPLOYEE_NAME)
FROM EMPLOYEE
GROUP BY DEPT

It will return
Finance: John, George, Smith, Julie
Marketing: Jim, Jack, Jasmine

31. How can we get the results from a table in a random order in MySQL?

We can use ORDER BY RAND() clause in SELECT query to get the results in a random order in MySQL.

Eg. SELECT * FROM EMPLOYEE ORDER BY RAND();
Above query will return the records from EMPLOYEE table in Random order.

32. How can we prevent duplicate

records in a MySQL table?

We can use these options to prevent duplicate records in MySQL table:

I. **Primary Key**: We can define a Primary key in a table. While entering data if there is already a record present with same Primary key, then duplicate record will be rejected.

II. **Unique Index**: We can also create a Unique Index on a column in a table. While inserting new data, if we use duplicate data then Unique index will throw error.

33. How will you eliminate duplicate values from a query result in MySQL?

MySQL provides DISTINCT keyword to remove duplicates from a query result. With DISTINCT keyword, a value will be displayed only once.

Eg. SELECT DISTINCT NAME FROM EMPLOYEE;

This query will return each name in Employee table only once.

34. How will you get the size of data in a MySQL table?

In MySQL, there is an information_schema that contains the TABLES object. We can run a query on TABLES to get the size of data in a table.

Eg. If we have a table named EMPLOYEE, the query to get the size of data will be as follows:

```
SELECT table_name "Table Name",sum( data_length + index_length ) / 1024 / 1024 "Table Size (MB)"
FROM information_schema.TABLES
WHERE table_name='EMPLOYEE';
```

35. What is the option in Amazon Web Services for MySQL?

Amazon Web Services provides a MySQL compatible database product named Aurora.

Amazon Aurora with MySQL is claimed to be five time faster performance than regular MySQL.

It is a high end commercial grade relational database based on MySQL. It is very cost effective as compared to other enterprise databases.

36. How can we manage multiple MySQL servers?

MySQL provides MySQL Enterprise Monitoring

and Advisory Service to manage multiple servers. We can monitor health, security, availability and performance of multiple MySQL servers from a consolidated dashboard with this service.

It also shows color coded charts that help in finding and resolving issues quickly.

37. How will you migrate your SQL Server database to MySQL?

We can use MySQL Workbench Migration Wizard to migrate Microsoft SQL Server database to MySQL DB. This wizard can also migrate Microsoft Access DB to MySQL.

38. What is the difference between MySQL and Oracle?

Some of the main differences between MySQL and Oracle are as follows:

I. **Authentication**: In MySQL there is an additional field location that is used for user authentication. Location parameter generally contains hostname, IP address or a wild card.

II. **Privileges**: In MySQL, privileges given to users and groups are in hierarchical system. Privileges available at a higher level are also granted to lower levels in same hierarchy.

At lower levels there is also an option of overriding the privileges passed from higher level.

39. What is the order of privileges in MySQL?

In MySQL, there is a hierarchical system of privileges. The order is as follows:

- Global
- Host Level
- Database Level
- Table specific
- Column specific

For each of these levels there is a separate grant table in the MySQL database.

40. Is it ok to mention a table name in lower case while creation and in uppercase while retrieving data from MySQL DB?

MySQL is a case sensitive platform. We have to specify the object names in same case all the times. Generally on all the Unix based platforms MySQL enforces case-sensitive rule for object names. In Microsoft Windows based installation MySQL does not enforce case-sensitive rule.

So it is always safe to use same case for Object names in CREATE and SELECT queries.

We can also use system level parameter lower_case_table_names to set the correct option for case-sensitivity in MySQL.

41. Why this query does not work in MySQL?

mysql> SELECT * FROM my_table WHERE MY_TABLE.col=1;

Unlike other databases, MySQL is case-sensitive in most of the platforms. In the above query we are using my_table and MY_TABLE to refer same table. This is not allowed in MySQL.

42. What is mysqldump?

MySQL provides a data backup utility called mysqldump. We can use it for creating logical backup of a database. Logical backup is a set of SQL statements that can be executed to recreate the database with original object definitions and table data.

mysqldump can also be used to create database

dump in csv, xml, json etc formats.

43. What is the limitation of mysqldump?

Since mysqldump is a logical backup it is not useful for taking backup of a database with large tables. mysqldump loads an entire table's data in memory before writing it to dump. Since memory is a limited resource, it is not a scalable option for dumping large tables.

In such a scenario, it is preferable to take physical backups of data.

44. Can we run Javascript or Python code in MySQL?

MySQL provides a tool called mysqlsh to run Javascript or Python code in a MySQL shell. We can use it to execute the code from Javascript and Python.

On calling mysqlsh, a new shell is created within regular shell. In the new shell we can write and run Javascript/Python code.

45. What are user-defined variables in MySQL?

In MySQL we can create user-defined variables. We can store a value in a user-defined variable in one statement and later use it in subsequent statements.

User-defined variables are specific to a session. A user-defined variable can not be shared among multiple clients.

The name of user-defined variable can have maximum 64 characters and it is case-insensitive.

46. How will you optimize a SELECT query in MySQL?

We can use following options to increase the speed of a SELECT query in MySQL:

I. **Index**: We can create index on the columns that are used in WHERE clause of SELECT statement.

II. **Function Isolation**: We can check whether a function is being called multiple times or one time. By isolating the specific function that takes longer time in a query, we can optimize it to improve the overall performance of a query.

III. **Full Table Scan**: Wherever possible we should minimize the full table scan in a query. We can use optimal WHERE clause to do this.

IV. **Table Statistics**: MySQL has an in-built optimizer that can optimize a sql query. But it needs current statistics from the table. To keep the statistics up to date we can run ANALYZE statement on a table.

V. **Memory**: We can also adjust the size and properties of Memory area to optimize the execution of a query in MySQL.

47. What are the different optimization techniques in MySQL?

Some of the optimization techniques in MySQL are as follows:

I. **Range Optimization**: In this case we can use a single index to retrieve the subset of data from a table. Now the server has to work on less amount of data.

II. **Index Optimization**: In this method several range scans can be merged into one result. So index scans from same table can be merged into one dataset.

III. **Engine Condition Pushdown Optimization**: When we have a direct comparison between a non-indexed column and constant, MySQL optimizer will push the condition to storage engine for evaluation.

I. **Index Condition Pushdown Optimization**: This is another optimization for selecting rows from a table by using an index.

48. How can we optimize INSERT query in MySQL?

We can use following techniques to optimize INSERT queries in MySQL:

I. **Values**: For inserting multiple rows in a table we can pass multiple VALUES as a list in an INSERT statement. It is faster than using single row INSERT per statement.

II. **Default**: If we have default value set on a column then we should not try to insert default value. We can just insert data with non-default value.

III. **LOAD_DATA_INFILE**: We can use LOAD_DATA_INFILE to insert data from a text file into MySQL.

49. How will you make MySQL system secure against attackers?

We can use following best practices to make MySQL secure against attackers:

I. **Password**: Each MySQL account should have a password. Also the password should be strong enough so that it can not be cracked by an attacker.

II. **Unix account**: Only the Unix user account with read or write privileges should run the mysqld process.

III. **Root**: MySQL should not be run by Unix root user. Because any user with FILE privilege in MySQL will be able to create file as root user.

IV. **FILE privilege**: We should not give FILE privilege to non-administrative users in MySQL.

V. **PROCESS/SUPER Privilege**: Also it is not advisable to give PROCESS or SUPER privilege to non-administrative users.

VI. **SYMLINK**: We should not allow symlinks to tables in MySQL.

VII. **Connections**: We should limit the number of connections allowed to an account in MySQL.

50. How can you protect your MySQL server against Denial of Service attacks?

In a Denial of Service attack, a malicious user may load the server with so many unwanted requests that the system becomes very slow and almost unusable to most of the other genuine users.

We can use following techniques to protect our MySQL server against any Denial of Service attacks:

- We should modify dynamic URLs with %22 ("), %23 (#) etc.
- We should modify data type in dynamic URLs from number to character format.
- We should check the size of data before passing it to MySQL. If there is larger amount of data than the average size, it should raise red flag.
- We should use different users for application connectivity to database than the administrative user.
- We can also enable strict sql mode to enable system to be more restrictive of the values it accepts..

THANKS

If you enjoyed this book or gained knowledge from it in any way, then I'd like to ask you for a favor. Would you be kind enough to leave a review for this book on Amazon.com?

It'd be greatly appreciated!

REFERENCES

https://www.mysql.com/

http://dev.mysql.com/doc/

Made in the USA
San Bernardino, CA
04 April 2017